Dear You

memoirs of a lost penguin

NISHAT B. AHMED

DEDICATION

This is dedicated to you all for believing in me, for making me never lose hope and for always encouraging me to do what I love.

For my best friend, who has always been there for me as my motivation, my inspiration and my support.

Dear Habiba,

Congratulations for winning the giveaway! Thank you for all your support and I hope you enjoy reading this!

— N.A

CONTENTS

Acknowledgments

1	DEAR READERS	Pg. 9
2	DEAR YOUNGER ME	Pg. 26
3	DEAR THEM	Pg. 48
4	DEAR A	Pg. 64
5	DEAR US	Pg. 88
6	DEAR FUTURE	Pg. 106
7	DEAR YOU	Pg. 118

ACKNOWLEDGMENTS

First and foremost, I'm so grateful for having this opportunity to fulfil my dream and that would have never happened without God's help. Alhamdulillah for this journey.

Thank you to @InnerRambling for my book cover! It took a while choosing the right cover, but my girl came through for me when I needed her.

Thank you to those who motivated me throughout the process of writing Dear You, you know who you are, I wouldn't have been able to complete it without you.

- CHAPTER ONE -
DEAR READERS

Everyone has chapter they don't read aloud.
But here it is.
Inked on paper.
Ready for the judging looks and whispers.
Ready for exposure.

Ready for you.

DEAR READERS;

Ever had the feeling that you had so much to say but didn't know how to, or who to tell? Ever had moments of regret, what ifs and what was? Or moments of hurt, moments of happiness, moments of contemplation? DEAR YOU is a book of letters that have never been sent, never been read, never been talked about; letters full of thoughts that have been eating away at every individual at one point in our lives.

This isn't just memoirs of a lost penguin, this is everything we've failed to say.

We're all a little lost in a world that is only temporary. This world was designed to break our hearts, don't you see? We try to find our feet, searching for all the right things but instead we come across the harsh reality. We search for what makes us happy, reading posts that we can relate to. When the people around you don't have a clue as to what you're going through.

We tend to forget that we're not alone, we're all just trying to find a place to call home. Not even the simplest of things is easy; nothing comes to you on a plate. You have to work for what you want, in order to elevate. In order to change this state that you've put yourself in. As I sit here and contemplate, I realise what it is that draws people in. The shining light, the calm after the storm; it's what everyone yearns for. Maybe they'll find it in my writing, maybe they'll hear it in my voice. Maybe they'll tap into my thoughts and find the hope they were looking for.

Whatever it is my dear readers, I hope this reassures you that you aren't alone.

To follow one's dream takes determination. It takes motivation. It takes willpower. For me to achieve my lifelong dream would mean much more than I can describe. The support I've constantly been getting from family and friends just to achieve that one dream of mine is endless. I cannot express how grateful I am to be given this opportunity.

If I can achieve this dream of mine; one I've worked so long and so hard for, so can you. You can do anything you put your mind to. You must want it. You must dare to dream. You must strive to do the best you can do. But most importantly, you must have faith in yourself. You must have faith in your abilities. Because without faith and hope, you'll fail to believe that what you'll achieve will end in success.

So dream big. Dream as much as you want. But never fail to put effort in for what you really want.

Go out there and get it.

What some of us fail to realise is life is too short. As cliché as it may sound, it's true. We either spend too much time dwelling on the past or we focus more on our future. Sometimes it's good to live in the present. We forget about the little moments that later become precious to us; we disregard them and later look back thinking what we could have done. In a flash, years go by and we wonder how it went that quickly. Why didn't we stop, and take it all in? Why didn't we embrace those moments while we could? While we still can? In any given moment, everything could change. Do we really want to live our lives this way, or is there a few things we'd alter to our liking so we could just enjoy it all a bit more?

True happiness is accepting that there will always be bad memories from the past and being able to look forward and focus on the now. Live everyday knowing what's happened, can't be changed. Make the most of every moment you have, before it's too late.

Know your self-worth. Stop putting others before you when you know they won't do the same for you. You are just getting yourself hurt for no reason when you could have just stopped this pain. Once you realise this, you'll know you deserve better than how you are being treated. Love yourself. Treat yourself better, and things will change for the better. You'll be happy, and that's the only thing that matters.

Sometimes having hope is the only thing that gets you through it all.

Don't focus on what is expected of you. Focus on what you expect of yourself. Only then will you achieve success and be happy in all that you do. Pleasing others gets you nowhere if you're not satisfied with yourself.

Don't ever make someone your first priority because chances are you're not theirs.

I believe deep down people write what their souls are destined to do. Now, you seem confused. Let me break it down and explain it to you.

People who write of love are nowadays mocked for expressing the same soppy emotions that they apparently can't get enough of. But it's not the truth. People who write of love have hearts of gold. They'll shower endless amounts of love to anyone that comes into contact with them. They'll show the world what love really is and people will crave to have a love just like what they write about.

People who write of heartbreak are scolded for being too depressed and repeating the same old thing. But these beautiful people are in actual fact helping the rest of the world cope with the emotions that are now mocked.

People who write about motivation and patience are special people who the rest of the world look up to. Maybe those same writers write about it to cope with the world themselves, and don't realise how much they help. Because you do, you help so much.

People who write about war and politics from all over the world; they aren't snobs or know-it-alls. Thank you, because you're informing this somewhat ignorant generation that there's a life outside of themselves and their boxes of comfort. There's hardship, in places we are unaware of, with things the media failed to portray.

People who write about human rights, rights of women and rights of men. Yes, it may not apply to you, but it apples to others. And we must be aware of what we are entitled to, no matter what. We must not be deprived of what's rightfully ours.

People who write about taboo subjects, things people fear to talk about, or are too shameful to acknowledge;

you are giving a voice to things that should be talked about. Sex offences, drugs, and domestic violence are only examples where we feel we can't talk about it. But why can't we? And those who write about it, are telling people it's okay. It's okay to speak out, it's okay... don't be afraid.

So do you see what I'm saying?

Writers provide the comfort for different things.

They write what their souls are destined to do.

I heard somewhere, "Darkness never wins. It just fools you into thinking it does." So why do we not fight back? Why do we give into the darkness when we know we are stronger than that?

Why do we forget that light will always prevail?

Life works in mysterious ways.
You may not get what you want right now, but later
you'll realise you got what you need.

Dear readers,
I think we forget not everyone has the same heart as
you. Not everyone has the same urgency to look after
someone dear to them or check in on someone they
haven't talked to in a long time. We think that because
we are caring and considerate towards others, the rest
of the world is the same. But that is not the case. Even
the closest of your friends may not ask after you or call
you in your time of need. And that's when you realise,
rather than relying on others you must rely on yourself.
Give yourself the love and the care that you would have
given to another. Take care of yourself so that you are
able to come out stronger and happier because of
yourself. Don't rely on others when they're not even
considering you until they need something.

DEAR YOU

- CHAPTER TWO –
DEAR YOUNGER ME

DEAR YOUNGER ME;

There's so much to say, so much that could have gone differently. There's memories, regrets and wonderings about every moment of our lives. So much has changed, and it's scary to think how quickly it all happened. As I think and reminisce, I am reminded of the times we all thought we had life figured out. The times where we thought that we'd finally have control over our future. The times where we thought we had gotten everything right. I am reminded of the friends, lovers, acquaintances we've left behind. I am reminded of the hurt, the long sleepless nights, the crying. I am reminded of the spontaneous trips, the laughter, the madness. And I think to myself, 'where has the time gone?' Where has the time gone. Time has run away with itself and we are left wondering what we could have done better; what we could have done. Regrets, wonderings, thoughts – they all eat away at us with the idea of what could have been. We are stuck in motion; remembering all we have said and promised ourselves what we'd never allow to happen. Then how is it we are here now, with all these memories and lessons? Things we should have seen coming but refused to acknowledge until it was too late.

It's too late.

There was once a girl who dreamt of all things young girls do at that age. She dreamt of princes and castles and 'happily-ever-after's. She was oblivious to the reality that surrounded her simply because she believed everything will work out in the end. She wanted her life to turn out like those books she read endlessly and those movies she couldn't stop watching. But dear child, do you not know life is not like it is in the movies? Everything is not what it seems but she didn't take consider this while she kept dreaming big; wishing for things she knew deep down would not come true. Life laughed at her and threw things at her from all corners. But Hope never left her side; constantly showering love over her. As the girl grew, she saw the best in everything, and saw beauty in things people failed to take a second look at. So when Love came along, giving the girl what she wished for, Life was ready. And it hit her. It hit her hard. Not everything is as it seems. Intentions are everything, and not everyone has good intentions. What hurts most is that not everyone has the same heart as you. They will do whatever to look after themselves and they will not even consider your feelings. And so the girl's spirit started to break, as she saw the reality of things. Life was cruel and there was nothing she can do. So she made the most of what she had, and left everything in the past.

14

A 14-year-old,
Lost in this world.
No one to look up to;
No guidance on what to do
Or how to live.
When writing became her motive;
A reason to go on, to get it all down.
A sense of belonging, she had finally found.

WHO AM I

I'm not who you think I am.

Makes you think, doesn't it?
Who am I?
What are my intentions?
Why did I just say that?
We are all quick to make assumptions without
explanations and that just leads to confusion. The only
way to avoid confusion is confrontation. Be careful, for
confrontations are the cause of arguments and then
there is nothing but debris of what used to be. The
aftermath of a battle; the remains of the lost.

Who am I?
You ask me if I know. You ask me as if I've got it all
figured out. Nothing is concrete and I am changing
every day. I am moulding into the person I should be,
without interference by those who are quick to judge.
Forget them all. Let them fight their own battles within
themselves.

Dear younger me,
I wanted to remind you what I used to write at a young age; how I got into writing, my Raxstar phase *dramatically rolls eyes* I was pretty dramatic back in those days; the young naïve Nish, that believed in fairy tales, that wished for a Prince Charming and a happy ending. That believed in the best of every situation, no matter how hard it got.

But it all started with my homework diary in 2002; my teacher used to make us write about our days to practice our writing skills. If it wasn't for her giving us a homework diary and my love for reading, I wouldn't have been into writing. So here it goes, a trip down memory lane.
(P.S. I included this just for laughs because I found this hilarious)

(2002):

Staying in houses

On Saturday I went to my aunty's house to stay.
Because I want to go. My mum said go away I cried. I
packed my racksack with lots of clothes. My aunty's
twins are nice.

The sad story

My nana was living and evrey one cried. I cried in the
airport. When I drink cokercola they chekd my nana.
She cried to. I said. Phone me. The others said phone
me. We began to fayt. And that was the end of the
storry.

Living

When my mum went to the kichin a man came to our door. He put the letur in the box. I got the leter from the box. I was reeding the words. Then mum came. She got the leter. Reeding it. She told ereybody. We was happy. Then she told our next door nabor. Shw went about 1, 6, minits she came back befor I rot about liveing. The End.

(This diary entry was about me and my sister finding about we were moving from my mum. And we were happy about leaving apparently.)

My luckiest day

When my dad brout a pen. He gave it to me. I said thank you in the car. When we got home my sister was rude. My mum said dad will hit her. Because she wrote on her legs while mum was cutting her nails. I was watching corranatian street and my sister being nautiey. Then she took off her underpants and she puts the underpant on. The End.

(I couldn't deal with this one, it's just too hilarious. I don't even know how I got away with writing this in year one.)

Anyway... I hope you enjoyed those embarrassing entries as much as I did. Fast forward to 6 years later, when I went on a residential in Kent with my year 6 class.

(JULY 2008)

My best memory of Gorsefield (Year 6 residential):
My best memory of Gorsefield was actually going there. At first, I was so excited but when it came to going, I became nervous and I didn't want to go. I am glad I did go. I really miss Gorsefield and I would do anything, absolutely anything, to go there again. I know that there have been bad times when people had gotten upset or homesick but I will always remember the good bits as well as the bad. There are many ways of making bad things into good, e.g. when you're lonely in the night, you can go to your friend's bunk so you can talk to them. They are the next best thing when your family isn't there. They are like your family.

(JUNE/JULY 2010)

So... these were during my 'Raxstar' phase. You can probably tell from the rhyming *dramatically rolls eyes* I really thought I was some bad ass punk. Judge me all you like, I was 14 years old, a teenager that thought they were badass. But it helped shape me into the person I am today.

I can't remember how I discovered Raxstar, but his songs were filled with emotion and passion. And I wanted to do the same too. I wanted to make an impact with my words. At that age, I dint know how I was going to do that. I only knew it was going to help me express what I was feeling and make sense of it all.

I looked up to Raxstar quite a lot, I don't know why, but he was my inspiration throughout my teenage years. He gave me a reason to never stop writing, to follow my dreams and I'm glad I did.

#1

You were my best friend, I didn't think it would end. You chose him over me, how can this be? You don't think you've done wrong, when that's what you've been doing all along. You know what he's done, so why are you being so dumb? I gave you my trust. Clearly that didn't last. You don't even know what he's like. This time, I'm the one that's right. Girl, are you in for a long ride. Either way, you'll never have me by your side. But you don't believe me. It's a living nightmare. It ain't a fairytale dream. But you really don't care.

(On a side note... she turned out to be a lying, cheating snake and they broke up a year or two later. So, thank goodness, I stayed away from both of them because who knows how things would have turned out now if I was still friends with either of them.)

#2

My life is messed; it's all a test. Every step I take, every move I make, I'm being watched. I'm getting touched by the devil. This was my mistake, every minute that I'm wasting. Every day there's new directions. Different paths in every section. I've become so selfish. I've become so mean. I've really changed. My only wish is to sort myself out, not scream and shout. Forget about him, forget about her. There's a chance that's very slim that things will go back to the way they were. At the end of the day, no one's going to help. There's only one way. You look after yourself.

(Damn... 14-year-old Nish, why you so deep for?)

#3

I wanna do what's right; I'm in the tunnel, but where's the light? Is it too late? Do I just wait? For the right time, with the right state of mind. I don't know what to do, can somebody just give me a clue? My mind's in different places, running different races. Every day I'm meeting new faces, in this life I'm just wasting.

(2015):

DROWNING

I find myself struggling to breathe, trying to get air into
my lungs;
But I am drowning, drowning.
You are the water, keeping me tightly wrapped and
suffocated;
And I am drowning, drowning.

I reach out for someone to help me,
But no one will save me, save me.
I feel myself giving up as I know,
No one will save me, save me.

I look around the room at everyone I thought were my
own,
And they are watching, watching.
They see me at my worst; ready to self-destruct,
And they leave me.

FALL

Mesmerised by your beauty, I have no words.
Your eyes shine like the stars;
Sparkling, as they make contact with mine.
Your smile is enough to light up my day.
You whisper sweet nothings in my ear,
And I find it hard to believe – is this real?
You act so mysterious,
I find myself wanting to know more.
You give me nicknames,
I pretend I don't like it but really, I do.
I feel myself getting attached.
I worry,
That I'll fall,
And you won't be there to catch me.

We're so busy trying to fix everyone around us and making them happy that we forget we're humans too. We're not machines. We need happiness too. Maybe we need fixing. And if no one will do it for us, we should focus on ourselves more; put ourselves first for once.

ELEPHANT IN THE ROOM

We look at each other and stop ourselves from
mentioning it.
Because we know once we notice it, it'll all fall apart.
Once the secrets are unravelled, everything pours out
into the open.
Instead, we sit here idly waiting for the elephant to
leave. Or are we?
The intentions of others are unknown
And the unknown is terrifying, for they could unravel
Things which could destroy us all.

Dear younger me,

We've come a long way from writing in notebooks and writing to stop the demons in our heads. I've become stronger than I thought I would be; I've gone from facing the demons in my head to facing real demons in my life. But the hope I've had, the faith that has kept me going, all stemmed from you; without your dreams and without the love you've had within yourself, I would have never been able to get this far. I would have never been able to help myself through the hardships of life. And to this day, I look back at the times of having homework diaries at the age of 5, writing stories throughout primary school and reading books to further develop my interest in literature.

I look back at my 'Raxstar' phase, and I see how much it had helped me express myself when I felt as if I had no one to talk to. I rediscovered my love for writing whilst listening to Raxstar and at times, it did help. The reason why I emphasize so much about this phase even now, is that it helped me so much with my feelings and expressing them the way I wanted to. I didn't hold back. I let it all out, and I felt good. I was 14, trying to make sense of everything at such a young age, not knowing that I was dealing with something greater than myself. I remember my Wattpad days, writing stories but never finishing a single one due to demotivation. Honestly, if it wasn't for the way I was, I wouldn't have got to where I am now; content with the lessons I've learnt and ready for whatever life throws at me. I know I am destined for great things, I have that much faith in myself. I've finally finished what I started, and it's lead to me so much more.

So, thank you. Thank you for never losing hope.

Write a letter to your younger self; reflect on your past and let go of any memories that is preventing you from living your present.

DEAR YOU

- CHAPTER THREE –
DEAR THEM

DEAR THEM;

You thought I wouldn't make it. You thought I wouldn't get this far. And quite frankly, I stopped believing in myself at one point. But I'm here. I got to this point. I got to achieve my dream even when people said it was a pointless dream. So what if it was a pointless dream to you? For all that know me well know how much I wanted to make something of myself through my writing and now that I have an opportunity, I will make the most of it.

This chapter is for all the people who think you can't make it in life, who keep putting you down because once they see you achieving your dreams, they'll realise what idiots they were. They'll realise their mistakes and by then it'll be too late, because you've reached the point where you're focusing on your happiness and it doesn't include them.

But remember, haters will always hate. It's what you do with all that negative energy that counts; you convert it into positive energy and hopefulness for yourself to grow and learn from it all. That's what matters. Your happiness is more important.

Dear them,

I don't even know what to call you; those who have wronged me? Those who mistreated me? Those who were good at putting me down?

I know, I wasn't the popular kid in school. To be frank, I'm glad. I didn't want to associate myself with you either. I saw and heard how you treated others and I didn't want friends like that. I knew you all but I knew best not to get too close. You were savages, pouncing whenever you got the chance.

I don't know if any of you will end up reading this, or realise it's about you, but a lot of you hurt me with your words. I believe it wasn't always intentional. I get that. But it still hurt. You still broke a little girl's self-esteem. I may not have been someone you'd normally associate with popularity, but I wasn't horrible to anyone. And I guess my caring nature was always taken for granted. But I learnt, that not everyone is kind and caring, not everyone will have the same heart as you do. It takes time to accept that, when you feel like you're being mistreated for no reason. But there'll come a time where none of that will matter. None of those people will mean much to you. They'll just become memories of what once happened.

I guess I never really fit in anywhere; a misfit, even now. I was a dreamer, dreaming of things beyond my reach but holding onto the hope that one day things will be in my favour.

I don't know where I'd fit in in the categories of high school. But you can call me a drifter. A lost penguin trying to find her way. I guess we're all a little lost really. We're all trying to find our way in life. We'll all go through different experiences during our lifetime, trying to figure out what to do.

Is it really about fitting in, or is it about finding your feet? Finding your purpose in life. Because to me, that's the only thing that matters; to find my purpose in life and fulfill it the best I can.

Dear them,

There's too many of you to name and too many that do not deserve importance to be named.

This is simply to show that all the hurt you once put me through, everything you did, may have been a big deal when we were younger. It may have seemed extreme. If you look at the bigger picture, your existence in my life means absolutely nothing.

What once felt like the end of the world, a drama that intrigued everyone, is now childish and meaningless. All those rivalries and popularity; has it done you any good now? Do people even care about that now?

Yes, at a young age, some people think it is everything. They spend most of their school lives trying to reach up that social ladder and all for what? What do you really gain out of it? A few years later, people drift apart, and are at different stages in their life. Who cares who you were in school?

What matters is who you become in the real world.

How you approach a situation determines your character. How you treat others shows your compassion or lack of. Treat others the way you like to be treated. It's all been said before, but people forget to acknowledge this when the situation arises. People forget to take others into consideration. One day, a day will come, when life hits you back with the same intensity you put someone else through. And that's when you'll realise. And it'll be too late.

These are mere thoughts of a person who has been on both ends and has seen the consequences of her own actions. I've realised my mistakes and have tried to put things right. I know I've wronged. Some fail to realise their wrongdoings and continue to blame others for their actions. But what good will that do, if you avoid it? What will you gain?
Let me tell you.
At the end of the day all you'll have is a guilty conscience, unable to move forward with life without owning up to your mistakes. Without putting things right. Without a peace of mind.

You hurt me, I let you break me.

You mocked me and took me for granted, I said nothing. You lied to everyone about me, created rumours from nothing, and I still don't know why.

I think we'll never truly know why a person wants to or feels the need to hurt us. Instead of going against all our beliefs and getting them back for what they done, show them how much better you are without them. Show them the successful man or woman you are becoming. Show them you are above all this. You have no interest in what they do. Because that's all they crave. Attention. And without the attention you give them, without them feeding on it all, they'll have nothing else to do. And they'll realise how petty they are. They'll realise who the idiot really is.

You can say whatever you want. You can do whatever you want. But only I've got the power to disregard it all. I'm the one who's in control of my destiny, not you. Nothing can put me down and I will keep rising higher. I will fulfil my dreams and be all that I can be. Your words don't mean a thing. You don't mean a thing.

You.

You act as if you're on my side. You say you'll be there and then you go behind my back. You start spreading lies. You think I don't realise. You stab me in the back so easily, without a second thought. And then you apologise, like it's so easy. Acting all innocent. But no one's innocent in this world. No one does things unknowingly. Because you knew. You knew it all. Yet you hurt me.

There's some people in your life that you just know, you just know you don't belong with them. As much as you try to fit in, as much as you try to let things be, it just isn't enough. There's more differences than similarities. There's more clashes than we thought. As time passes by, you see they only contribute to putting you down rather than bringing you up. They're no longer a part of your happiness. And maybe that's how life is supposed to be played out. You win some, you lose some. It's not about how long you've known someone, it's about the impact they've had in your life. Time does not measure the strength of your bond nor will it measure the strength of your love. And once someone stops having meaning in your life, that's it. It's over. And there's nothing you can do to rectify it.

From the moment I met you, I saw the glimmer in your eyes. I saw the fire inside of you, waiting to get out. And all it took was one look, and you unleashed the monster inside you. You calculated your every move, waiting and watching. Watching me like a hawk. You waited for the right moment and pounced on me like a lion. You roared until you got what you wanted. And all I could do was let you. I let you destroy me.

To build ourselves up, we must let go of all negativity;
let go of the past and carry on pushing forward to reach
our goals. And once we start we must never stop,
because our dreams are worth a thousand stars and not
a single one should go to waste.

Dear them,

It took me a while to get to where I am now. It took a lot of strength too. And I am not letting anyone take it all away from me. I am not letting you destroy it all.

People admire the way I am now, but they don't realise how many people have attempted to destroy me in the process of it all. People I thought were good, people I trusted hurt me in so many ways yet I carried on without them. Life goes on.

I told myself the last time, "no more." I told myself that this would be the last time I let anyone come close to me, the last time I let anyone hurt me. And to this day I stand true to my oath.

Yes, everything in the past had lead me to this moment. I am grateful to have this moment. But if I had a choice to still have this moment and not go through betrayal, I would take it in a heartbeat. Who wouldn't? But I will not allow anyone else do what they once did to me. I will not get hurt.

So take your best shot. Give it all you've got. But you won't see me hurting. You won't see me breaking because of you.

I'll never give you the power to do so.

VENT.
Vent all you want.
Write whatever is on your mind.
Let it all out, because once it's out it can't get to you
anymore. It can't hurt you. Only you have the power to
let it. So don't. Don't let it hurt you.

- CHAPTER FOUR –
DEAR A

DEAR A;

We've all had that one person in our lives, that no matter what we simply can't let go of. There's something always drawing you together. We all have that one person, or we are that person.

Dear A is a chapter about that one person. It's about struggles of every kind of relationships. It's about compromise. It's about knowing what you want. It's about giving someone the power to hurt you but hoping they don't. It's about the effort you put in to something, trying to preserve what you have. It's about knowing when to let go.

Someone once told me, "Most people will hurt you, especially the ones you value the most. Then it's a case of is it worth being hurt by them; do they make my life better or worse and does the good and happiness outweigh the bad?" This is all about figuring out what happiness you get out of it, if any. And to embrace all that is and let go of all that was. This is about learning when enough is enough and realise there's nothing you can do to stop the oncoming storm.

Dear A,

I guess, to understand what happened, and what went wrong, we must start at the beginning. The very beginning. When the penguin met the monkey. But we didn't have those nicknames then. You were just someone I barely knew.

We met in unusual circumstances, but this isn't about how we met. It's about how I fell in love with the guy who stole my heart and slowly crushed it. The broken pieces still remain with him to this day. And I'm sure you know this, A. There is no doubt in my mind that my heart will forever remain yours, no matter how much we both don't want it to.

But it wasn't always like this. You were once the most annoying person I had ever known. That hasn't changed because you still are, I've just learnt to embrace it. I remember talking to my friends about you. How you were so frustratingly annoying yet something about you had me intrigued; had me wanting more. No matter what anyone said, I didn't listen. There was this mystery about you. And I wanted to solve you. I wanted to get to know you. But I didn't realise until so much later, what a puzzle you turned out to be.

You were cute, funny and it didn't feel weird talking to you. It felt normal. It felt right. At that time, I knew there was something wrong. There was something quite off with you, but I couldn't quite put my finger on it. And I wasn't ready for another heartbreak. But I knew with you, it was inevitable. It was too good to be true. But I was ready for the rollercoaster of a journey I would have with you. I just didn't realise how much of a rollercoaster it would be.

Who knew that the young annoying guy I was trying to get to know would end up meaning so much to me? To be honest with you, I think back then I knew. I knew you'd be someone important in my life. Deep down, I wanted you to be. And as much as my friends warned me against you (more than several times, I'll have you know), I didn't listen. I refused to take anyone's opinions into consideration. I knew no matter who you were, and whatever you were hiding, I knew behind the front you put up, there was a good decent guy in there. Sometimes I do wonder what would have happened if I did listen to my friends - would I have been saved from all this heartache? Or was it written in the stars for my heart to be broken by you?

Forever yours,
Penguin x

P.S. that's just something I'm testing out.
P.P.S. do you like it?
P.P.P.S. I do.

Dear A,

You'll be surprised at how much I remember, even if it was three years ago. I have a horrible memory, yet I remember every conversation I had with you, every time I saw you in college, and the butterflies... I had butterflies every time I saw you. There was one thing that stopped me from talking to you in front of everyone. I was scared nothing would come out of my mouth and I'd stand there looking so awkward. For some reason, I felt like you were out of my league. I was heading into new territory and it was frightening.

Even then I knew, how different we both were. We had different career paths, different lifestyles. Our mindsets were different but it didn't mean we didn't learn from each other, because we did. We just had different perspectives on life, and it wasn't a bad thing. Your outlook on life was different, and yes, more realistic than mine but I was a dreamer. And I believed in my dreams working out, no matter how outrageous they were. And you were always there supporting each and every one of my dreams. Without that, this book wouldn't be possible.

But obviously things got a little complicated along the way (okay I lied; a lot complicated). Out of all the stupid high-school crushes I had, out of the stupid guys I fell for, this one felt more than a crush. It felt real. And that terrified me. You weren't ready for a relationship, and you wanted to stay as close friends for the time being.

And after thinking about it, I agreed. I didn't want something temporary because temporary meant losing you one day. So, I went along with it. And for a while it was alright. You were still the first person I talked to when I woke up and the last person I said goodnight to. And you called me princess. Every time you called me princess, my day got a little bit better. You made me smile. You made me feel like I was special. And I believed you.

I don't know whether that was me being stupid or me putting my full faith in you. I don't know what I was thinking. My judgement was clouded and I thought what I was doing was best.

But how long until something went wrong, and I felt like you didn't really care for me?
Answer: not too long.

It was inevitable, wasn't it?

Forever yours,
Penguin x

Dear A,

So, we come to the first time you broke my heart.

Are you ready?

Because I'm certainly not. Even thinking about it still hurts me to this day.

That night, I told you that maybe we shouldn't speak anymore and you didn't fight it. There were many reasons why I said what I said that night. I was sick of the mixed signals, trying to figure it all out when I never got a straight answer from you. But what got to me the most out of everything is when you said, 'what did you expect out of me?'.

That

Hurt

Like

Hell.

It really did.

I remember that night so clearly. I was in shock. Unsure of how to respond. Unsure of everything.

"What did you expect from me?"

I didn't expect much. I wanted consistency and honesty – how was that so much to ask of you?

"What did you expect from me?"

Not to be led on; hoping and waiting for something or

someone.

But what did you expect from me? I was constantly overthinking and my anxiety kept getting the best of me. I spent months with insomnia, wondering where it was I went wrong.
And yet you expected me to be okay with it all. You expected me to believe you. How could you expect that of me when you refused to acknowledge my expectations?

I don't think you even get how those seven words made me feel. I remember reading that line over and over in my head that night. I remember how I froze when I first read it. I didn't know what to make of it. And that was the first time I cried because of you. And it certainly wasn't the last.

And I've always told you, you've never given me a reason to think differently, and I still believe to this day, you don't understand how uncertain everything was for me. I still believe that you don't really fully understand what you put me through and how I was more than willing to work things out every single time.

But after a long talk we decided to just stay friends. Just friends. And I don't know how you never got this, but every time we talked it was more than friends. Friends don't talk like we did sometimes. We both know that. And I guess we were always overstepping the line. That was never going to change.

I still think about that day; why did things have to be so complicated? What would have happened if I didn't tell you I had feelings for you? I guess we'll never know now. But if I had the chance to go back, would I have not told you? Never.

Forever yours,
Penguin x

Dear A,

Now this was the time our friendship was really tested. This is one of the times I'm so grateful I had you when I needed you.

We had a family emergency and at this point you knew how I was like with stress. I could barely sleep as it is, and this made things worse. My health got worse as the days went on. I was scared to say the least. I had to stay strong, but I could feel myself breaking from trying to understand what was going on. I couldn't deal with the situation on my own.

Throughout this time, you were there, all night every night talking to me. You helped me get my mind off it all, you let me talk it out and you stayed up until I fell asleep. By now, my sleeping pattern was horrible; I was awake at random times, and I couldn't stop the overthinking. But I knew I had you, and I knew you'd help me overcome these feelings. So, every night, I looked forward to having those moments with you, no matter how short they were. I looked forward to those small moments of happiness, before the worries overwhelmed me the next morning. I don't know how, but I knew I could count on you. I knew you wouldn't let me deal with it on my own.

I realised I didn't want to lose you one day. I constantly made sure you got home safe, and you were okay. I was worried more now. I was thinking all sorts and my mind was only at ease when I knew you got back safe and sound. When moments like those happen, you realise what's important in your life, and it helped me realise that you were important to me. And I didn't want to lose you.

I had someone to confide in, someone that knew my worries and knew I was vulnerable, yet was considerate and caring. No one but you knew what was going on at that time, and I trusted you. I told you because I trusted you. I was at my most vulnerable, and I let you in. Do I regret it? No. I'm glad I told you, I'm glad I had you.

Since then, I knew, every time something happened, you would be the first I'd go to no matter what. Not because I had done so previously, but because I trusted you. I trusted you would know what to do or say, I knew you'd be there for me.

It's moments like these that make you forget the bad in someone. I'll always remember it, but I'll also always remember you helping, just by talking and getting my mind off it all. But is that enough? Is it enough to forget the heartache you put me through?

I guess we'll find out soon enough.

Forever yours,
Penguin x

Dear A,

And so, we come to the fifth letter, and the time before I left for Christmas break. There would be several times where I felt as if I was just being taken for granted. Or I was just too gullible. I believed every single one of your excuses when you told me you were busy, (believe me they get more outrageous as the years went by).

We talked about a lot of things, but it was just that. Talk. All talk, no action. You promised me things, and it's hard to forget it all. Because I thought it meant to you as much as it did for me. I don't know if it was me overthinking it all, maybe it was my insecurities, maybe I felt I wasn't good enough for you. And there were many times when I felt that way. It was confusing. And there was no clarity. No consistency. No certainty. No explanations. And that's all I ever asked for, but I never got. All you had to do was be clear, and everything would have made sense.

But I get it now, it was both our faults. We just weren't open with each other back then. I failed to express how I was feeling and you failed to tell me what it was you really wanted, without being cryptic. Without confusing me.

You see, by now, I know you're probably thinking there's so much more to what I am saying. And I know there was. It's just I never knew what it was. And I probably won't ever know. But this is my story, my side of what happened. And it's all truth. It's just, the truth hurts.

Up until now, I've blocked out every time you hurt me simply because it hurt to look back. It hurt to remember it all. It was easier remembering all the good memories.

At this point, we were still getting to know each other and my insecurities were worse than ever. And I guess it all was playing on my mind a lot. I kept thinking you could do better. I kept thinking I wasn't good enough.

You told me it was all about trust. And yes, I did trust you, but not completely. Not when it came to this. You had to give me a reason to trust you, an explanation for the way you were with me at times. I guess at that time, all I really wanted was an explanation. A confirmation of how you felt, if you felt anything. I wanted to know this wasn't going to be something temporary. I wanted to know something. Anything. I just wanted you to be open. And I couldn't get that from you. All you said was you can't stop me from doing anything, and you've said what you had to. Wrong answer, A. Wrong answer.

I continued to blame myself for being too insecure, for confusing myself that I didn't realise I was destroying myself in the process. I was talking nonsense, trying to make sense of it all. And looking back, I feel sorry for myself for feeling you were better off without me. Maybe we were better off without each other. Maybe we weren't. But it was no one's fault.

Why I didn't leave at that point, I don't know. It would have made things much simpler. No more confusion. But I was already in way too deep and way too attached to someone I didn't even plan to be.

I didn't know what to do. But we all know what I did. I left things as they were simply because I couldn't bear to leave. I couldn't lose you. But honestly, if I lost you then, I probably could have moved on. I could have forgotten you. I could have left you in the past instead of spending years trying to figure you out and ending up heartbroken.

But that's what I did, didn't I?

I let it go on. I set myself up to fall. And I fell. I fell hard.

I got over the fact that you were all talk, no action. I got over it for the sake of our friendship. Just to preserve what we had.

Was that a good move of mine? I don't know.

Forever yours,
Penguin x

Dear A,
I don't know why I struggled to say all this to you, why I
found it hard to tell you how I felt about it all. But I
guess my insecurities played a huge part. I wish I was
honest about how I felt, how you made me feel,
whether it was intentional or not.

But what I'm trying to say is, yes, I did get hurt, but we
did have good moments. You see, I didn't plan to fall for
you. I didn't plan to set myself up for heartbreak. It just
happened and it was just something I had been trying to
deal with on my own. I'd been trying to stay strong,
trying to preserve what we had, so I'd never lose you.
And I think that's what broke me more. I was trying so
hard to put my feelings aside that I couldn't focus on
what we had. I wanted more and it wasn't happening. It
just wasn't written in the stars for it to happen.

And I guess 'I want never gets.' Which is why, there
were times we spent apart due to my own frustration
and confusion that was going on in my head.

But that's for another letter.
Another letter, another piece of my heart I bare out.
Are you ready, A?

Forever yours,
Penguin x

Dear A,
You told me to write about how I felt when you weren't around. So here it goes.

Let's start with the times you suddenly disappeared off the face of the earth and came back with ridiculous excuses. I thought I did something wrong. Every time, I always blamed myself. I thought I said something or did something and beat myself up about it.

I spent days and nights wondering where it was I went wrong, what I did and how I screwed it up. Then it came to a point where my feelings turned into anger. I was being used and I let it happen to myself. I let you. I was done caring. I didn't believe a word of your excuses. Because something was up with you; I just didn't know what.

I don't know why or how I put up with it all. I just continued giving you the benefit of the doubt. I continued having faith in you, because I knew you had the potential to be good and do good.

And it's pretty clear how much I felt for you when we did spend time apart from each other. I felt empty. Without a part of me. And it felt weird. It felt wrong. I wasn't able to cope without you and I found it hard to do so.

I clearly remember the time when I had had enough and decided to put an end to it all. I remember giving you an ultimatum and telling you I couldn't deal with these childish antics of yours. Enough was enough. But I didn't realise the storm that followed after that. I felt like a part of me was missing and the overwhelming feelings got too much for me. I realised I didn't really mean much to you. Because if I did, you would have fought. You would have explained. You would have let me know what was going through your head, but you didn't. It took me a while to convince myself I could move on and leave it all in the past.

And as much as I thought I moved on, as much as I thought I was starting a new chapter in my life, I couldn't let go of your chapter. After getting my heart broken, months later, I found myself back to you. I found myself seeking solace in the one place I knew I would get it. Home. Because that's what you were. And that's all I had known for the few years. You were home, and I was homesick. And I found myself feeling better, and I didn't feel incomplete. I was whole again. And you helped me through it all. You were there helping me, motivating me to get back up and sort myself out.

I didn't want someone to have the power to hurt me anymore, and you had abused that power before. But you helped me so much, and you were there for me more than ever. I couldn't help but get attached. But I guess that proved I never really got over you? And I knew. I just knew something would go wrong; it doesn't take long for us but something always goes wrong.

I just hope fate has better plans for us, and for once something goes right instead of going wrong.

Forever yours,
Penguin x

Dear A,

You once asked me to write about you, and I felt it was too personal to share with others. My words held so much meaning. It was filled with regret with what happened, love from what we had and gratitude for all you'd done for me. So here it is, A.

You ask me to write about you, but what is it I'm supposed to say? What is it I'm supposed to say that I haven't already? My thoughts are exhausted with words I've said, words I've failed to say. Time has passed but you remain one of my closest friends to this day. You're frustrating at times, annoyingly funny and sweet. Your soul is as pure as nothing I've ever known. You bring me light to my dark days, and make me laugh when I need it the most. You get my weird quirks and accept the psycho in me. You understand me more than most. There's something about you I can't quite put my finger on but it's a feeling of familiarity, a feeling of peace. There's several things I could say but it's hard to tell someone how much you appreciate them. I remember telling you once how you were a mystery to me; and yes, there's parts of you I've yet to know but the parts I know are so sincere and caring. Quoting from one of my favourite books, "you never really understand a person until you consider things from his point of view, until you climb inside of his skin and walk around it" and that's how you know what they're really like. But in the time that I've known you, I've understood the parts of you you've chosen to show, if anything, and I do admire the changes in you I've seen. You've come a long way in terms of everything and it takes courage to acknowledge it and make a change to oneself. And I guess it's funny how time hasn't really changed a thing; you're still the annoying person I met all those years ago. Your friendship means more to me than I let on, it gives me peace knowing I have a friend like you and I'd never want that to go away. You're still the sweet soul who's always there for his friends. And I pray that never changes. And I pray you get all you deserve, and you are happy. I wish nothing but the best for you and your future, with hope that all your dreams do come true.

Forever yours,
Penguin x

Dear A,

I guess what I'm trying to say from all this, is that no matter what has happened between us, I'll never regret knowing you. I'll never regret a single moment. You were the first person I truly fell for and that's something I can never forget.

You're my best friend, my annoying best friend but I'd never change you. I'd never replace you for anyone else.

I don't know what will happen once you've read this, what you'll feel towards me; if you'll hate me for this. But whatever happens, I'll always cherish the moments we've had already. Whatever happens, I'll never forget you.

Forever yours,
Penguin x

Dear A,

When I'm with you, I feel like I'm 17 again; that awkward 17-year-old that's still trying to find her place in life. The one that didn't fall for your charm that easily but was still mesmerised by the mystery that lingered over you. That little girl who believed in love, in romance, in fairy tales. That her Prince Charming would come one day disguised as her best friend. And he did. She thought you were. And every time I think of you, I still believe you are. Were. I don't know. All I know is I do stupid and unexplainable things around you, and instantly kick myself for being such a child. But that's what we were at 17/18, when we met. We were still kids. Maybe that's why things didn't work out. We needed time to grow, away from each other. Maybe it won't ever work out, but I'll always remember how you made me feel. And maybe that will have to be enough.

Forever yours,
Penguin x

Dear A,

We can't change what's happened. But we can change what's about to happen. We can make the decisions that defines everything for us. Our stories are still being written. So write a good one you'll be happy with.

Nothing lasts forever, but I am grateful for the brightness you brought into my life. I can never forget that. You'll forever remain in my memories but like I've always said, it was inevitable.

I'll always believe in fate and things happening for a reason. I can honestly say that I met you for a reason. I wasn't sure why for so long. But I've known why for a while now. And I'm glad I met you. Because I wouldn't have learnt from it all. I wouldn't have come out stronger, happier and more independent. So thank you so much. Thank you for helping me become the person I am today.

Forever doesn't last forever.
Penguin x

Dear A,

Every person in our lives comes either as a lesson or blessing or maybe even both. There'll always be regrets, there'll always be what ifs. But it's whether you let them take over you that matters the most. Is it even worth thinking about? Or are you better off the way you are now?

Life will always throw obstacles at us, and these obstacles may come in the form of people.

There'll always be people we'll never forget, moments we'll always remember and memories we'll always relive. There's no doubt in my mind that we all have that one person that made everything better, the one person who knows you so well. The one person worthy of your love.

This chapter isn't necessarily about a certain person. It's about every person. Every one that entered our lives and made an impact on who we are and who we continue to be. It's about the story of friendship and love, and what matters the most. It's about sacrifice.

Maybe A was a mistake. Maybe not. We'll never know. But it happened, and it was over before it had begun. And maybe that's for the best.

- CHAPTER FIVE –
DEAR US

DEAR US;

Ever wondered what your future will be like? Who you'll end up with? What you'll do? Where you'll go?

Life is a mystery and it's always changing. We have the power to change it.

This chapter contains questions we all have in our minds, hopes we secretly wish for. We all want a happy ending. We all await the day, we can look back at our life and be content with the way it has turned out. We want that day where we're with our other half and we smile at them for no reason. Just glad that they're there. We all want that time where everything feels like it's in its place, when it all feels right.

DEAR FUTURE HUSBAND
DEAR DAUGHTER

I'm not looking for a person to fix me; to connect my broken pieces together. I'm looking for someone who holds my broken pieces gently and loves me regardless of the pieces that are hard to fix. I'm not looking for a person to get rid of all my bad days, I'm looking for a person who sits through each one with me and just lets it be. I'm not looking for the one that knows me instantly, inside and out. I'm looking for the one I can grow with as we go through new experiences in life. I'm not looking for a Prince Charming, a Mr. Perfect. I'm looking for a man who himself has flaws and embraces each and every one, who appreciates things that aren't usually appreciated. I'm looking for a man who supports me rather than belittles me. I want a friend who's there for me when he says he will be.

Search for the one who ignites the fire in your soul, who calms the storm in your head and claims your heart as his. And when you find him, never let go. Don't you ever let go of what could be the key to the fairytale ending you've always dreamt of.

Dear Future Husband,
I haven't met you yet, and I am in no rush to. I know whenever I do meet you, everything will feel like it will fall into place. Everything will make sense. Everything that happened was supposed to, because it will eventually lead me to you.

I haven't met you yet, but I know you will be everything I have ever dreamed of. You'll be the person I was always looking for. You'll be the reason for my happiness. And that happiness will last for a lifetime. I won't ever have to question your love for me. I won't have to question your words or your actions. Because everything will feel right. Everything will feel complete.

I know I'll get the happiness I deserve one day, and I know it will be with you. I have learnt so much over the years and it's made me more grateful for all the blessings in my life. That's why I don't mind waiting for you; because you'll be the biggest blessing in my life.

I can and I will be patient for you. I will wait. Because once you come into my life, I am never letting you go. I am never letting you leave me.

With love,
Your Queen.

Dear Future Husband,
I wonder when we meet, will I know instantly? Will I know that you're the one I will spend the rest of my life with?

I'd like to think my instincts are usually correct, so tell me, will my instincts kick in when I meet you? Will I feel everything I wanted to feel when I meet The One?

I wonder if you'll recognise me instantly. I wonder if you'll know that I'm the one for you? Or will it take time for us to realise we were meant to be?

I have so many questions, and I know that I'll get the answers to them in time. I have been patient all this time, I know I can be patient for a while longer. But it doesn't stop me wondering what you'll be like. Who you'll be. What you'll look like.

I wonder if you'll be the person I've been dreaming about; the one I can share my dreams with, the one who becomes my everything. I wonder if I'll find a best friend in you, if I can share my crazy thoughts with you, and spend my sleepless nights talking about anything and everything. I wonder if you'll understand me, and love me for who I am.

I wonder about you a lot, but only because I'm curious. Curious to know the one who'll soon know me better than anyone.

With love,
Your Queen.

Dear Future Husband,
When you make me yours, when you take me to my new home, will you vow to keep all the promises you make to me? Will you promise to protect me, to love me, to care for me?

Because I promise, that no matter what, I'll continue to shower my love to you for as long as we live. I promise to take care of you, to be your support, your motivation whenever you need me to be. I promise that whenever life feels hard, or it's getting you down, I will always be there to pick you back up. I'll be there encouraging your dreams, pushing you to be the best person you can be. I'll be there motivating you when you need it the most.

When you make me yours, will you do the same? Will you support my dreams and help me fulfil each and every one? Will you be the reason why I get up each morning with a smile on my face and the smile never ending because my thoughts are filled with you? Will you continue to make me smile, so I can go to sleep peacefully? Will you wait until I can sleep, and will you give me company the nights I struggle to sleep the most? Will you love my flaws and embrace them all?

You see, I have so many questions, so many wonderings about you. But I hope I never have to question your love for me, for I will always continue to love you the same.

With love,
Your Queen.

Dear Future Husband,
I hope like me, you can't wait for your first child. To go through the process of growing a baby inside you must be so magical. So special. But the suspense throughout it all must be so daunting. I hope you're as nervous as I am. To bring an innocent soul into this world for us to shape into a wonderful human being.

I can't wait till I see them in your arms, and you feeding them, putting them to sleep. Playing with them. I can't wait for it all. I can't wait to do it all with you.

When you finally meet your little prince or princess, when you see that small bundle of hope, I know it will change everything for you. Because now, you'll have someone looking up to you. A son, watching his father and learning to be just like him, or a daughter, learning that all men should be like her father.

But I have faith, that our children will love you unconditionally and immensely, just like I will. They will look up to you. and you will realise the responsibilities that lie ahead. It's okay to be nervous. It's okay to feel like you'll make a mistake.

We'll make mistakes, and continue to do so. But we'll learn from them. We'll teach them to love, to learn, to become strong independent people. We'll do it together.

With love,
Your Queen.

Dear Future Husband,
This is a reminder for you, one I hope you'll look back on in years to come. This is a reminder that I love you.

Now keep that in mind every time I act hastily or on impulse. Every time I say something stupid and instantly regret it. Every time I annoy you with my mood swings or weird nonsense that no one else gets. Every time I argue with you (I'm hoping that's basically never). Just remember I love you.

I know how difficult I can be at times. I know sometimes I like my own space and I want to isolate myself from the world. Be patient with me please. I hurt almost the same amount as I love. And it can be a tricky journey. But I know together, we can get through anything.

Even if people talk, and we know people talk; but even then, it doesn't matter. What matters most is you and I. There will always be someone that isn't happy, and there's nothing much we can do about that. It's not their relationship, it's ours.

So remember my love...Together, we can take on the world; together, anything is possible. I know I'm being cheesy right now, but we all need that once in a while, and here is yours. Here is that little piece of hope you can keep forever, reminding you that you'll always have me. I hope you never forget that.

With love,
Your Queen.

Dear Future Husband,
In 20 years from now, I hope we have achieved everything we have dreamed of. I hope we have the family we've dreamt of for years, I hope we are both successful in our careers, and I hope our love remains stronger than ever. I hope we are happy.

Nothing in the world would mean more to me knowing my family is happy, and I would do anything to see that happen. I hope you would do.

But if anything were to ever happen to me, if anything unexpected were to happen, I hope I can rely on you to look after the kids, to make sure they get the upbringing they deserve. I hope me not being there doesn't change anything. Because my love shouldn't be missed; you should be able to fill that hole in their lives. Give them a mother's love as well as a father's love.

It's not something to be thought about, but it must be thought about. You must be able to remain strong throughout it all. You must be, for the sake of the kids.

I hope nothing ever does happen to either of us; I hope we are able to witness our children growing up, into young adults with the world at their feet. But if anything should, if anything should happen… you must be able to carry on. You must give them the life we always wanted for them. Give them love. Give them hope. Give them what they need.

With love,
Your Queen.

Dear Daughter,
I can't wait to hold you in my arms, my little baby. I can't wait to see you, to finally have a little piece of hope, a little piece of your father and I.

I've been dreaming of you since I was little, wondering how you'd look, what you'd be like, who you'd look like. What features from the family you'd inherit. I hope you inherit strength and courage from your elder aunt, selflessness from your youngest aunt and endless love and protectiveness from your uncle. They're a bunch of mad people, but those qualities they have are the best qualities and I'd want you to have them.

You'll always have a part of me and your father in you, no matter what. And I don't know what you'll get from both of us, but I hope it's all the best qualities. I hope they help you get through anything. I hope these qualities guide you to do the right things in life.

I know you'll bring the family so much happiness, and I hope that never changes. I have so much hope for you and who you'll become.

Lots of love,
Mum.

Dear Daughter,

I can't wait for the adventures that lie ahead with you. I can't wait to take you to zoos, aquariums, parks. I can't wait to show you places and see your eyes widen from excitement. I can't wait till you're old enough to do all that.

More importantly, I can't wait till you learn to start crawling, walking, speaking. I want to be there every step of the way, helping you and guiding you. I want to see the smile on your face from accomplishing it all.

I know there'll be late nights, maybe even no nights with sleep. I know there'll be times where you'll be grumpy (I hope you don't take after me) and there'll be times where you'll be grizzly. But I honestly can't wait for it all. I know that with having a baby comes with great responsibility and I know when I have you, I'll be ready for it. And even if I'm not, I'll get used to it, and just seeing you in my arms will make it all worth it.

I'm looking forward to spending the rest of my journey with a family of my own, and I am excited. I hope you'll enjoy it as much as I do.

Lots of love,
Mum.

Dear Daughter,

It won't be too long till it's time for you to go to secondary school. Years will fly by and I'll be wondering how you've already grown up so much with a blink of an eye. And from then on it'll feel like you're just growing up way too fast for my liking.

But these years are the most important years of your life. Not in the sense of socializing, but performing academically. I want you to be able to excel in all that you do, put your full focus and 100% effort in everything. I want you to have the opportunities I didn't have, because of my lack of effort and focus. I want you to put yourself out there, be in every club you want to be in, every after-school activity that speaks to you. Anything that you know will help you, regardless of what your peers might think. I want you to make the most of secondary so that you open doors for many opportunities before and after college.

You have it in you to be great, so take every opportunity to prove yourself.

Lots of love,
Mum.

Dear Daughter,
There'll come times when you'll believe what people
say rather than wait for them to act. You'll care for a
boy who takes you for granted, or he'll treat you badly.
You'll feel so hurt and confused as to why he's being
like that.

That's when I'll tell you, that it's not worth it. That he's
not worth it. Why waste tears over a boy who can't see
how amazing you are, and settle for something you're
not happy with?

I'm saying this because I know, at least once in your life,
you'll be heartbroken. You'll know what it's like to give
but never be able to take. Not properly. And he will hurt
you. But you can't let him. You can't let him. I won't let
you let him.

You're a teenager and you'll think you know what love
is. You'll think it's something cute and everyone wants a
taste of it. But it's not what you think it is. Not
everything is as it seems. Love isn't airy-fairy nonsense.
There's a lot to love, that you'll only understand once
you get older. And you'll realise that the boy you cried
over once upon a time, was nothing. His existence was
nothing.

So don't worry about a thing, my love. Because when
the time comes, you'll find the perfect one. You'll find
him. But for now, just live your life. Live it and enjoy it.

Lots of love,
Mum.

Dear Daughter,
This will be my last letter to you.
My last letter to somehow advise you, give you an insight into how I'm feeling and thinking. But I guess we have plenty of time when we meet. We'll have years to come.

So, in my last letter, I just want to tell you that things will happen in life, unexplainable things. Things no one will have answers for, and that's okay. It's okay not to have answers. And it's okay to have questions. Ask questions. And go looking for answers. Go searching for the things that mean the most to you.

But never lose yourself in the process of searching for happiness. If anything, you'll find it within yourself. So be happy in all that you do, and you'll always have me by your side, regardless of it all.

Lots of love,
Mum.

Dear us,
There's a lot to look forward to, there's a lot of hope to
be had. And there's a lot of time left for all of that to
happen. Because whenever it does happen, it'll all
happen at the right time.

Things will not go as planned, that's a given. But it'll all
happen in our best interests. So don't give up hope just
yet, there's more years to come. There's so much left to
do. So brace yourself. And get ready for this journey.

Everything is uncertain right now, and maybe that's for
the best. Don't overthink it, and just let it all flow. Chase
your dreams and let the rest unfold.

DEAR YOU

- CHAPTER SIX –
DEAR FUTURE

DEAR FUTURE;
We all wonder who we'll be in years to come; if we'll
achieve the goals we set for ourselves. If the dreams we
have now comes true. If things will go the way we
wanted it to go...

I guess we'll only know if and when the time comes.

But for now, hold on tight. Just watch the future unfold
in front of you and wait for the things you deserve.

Dear Future,

I wonder how things will be like in 5 years' time. Will my career be what I've always dreamed of? Will I be married? Will I have the life I've always wanted? So many questions when it comes to the future but nothing's ever certain.

From a young age, there was nothing more I wanted to do than be a writer. I wanted to work within that field, doing what I love doing. I love books, and that has been my passion for so long. Even if I wasn't writing, if I was editing or publishing books, that would be the best thing ever. Will I get to fulfil that dream of mine? Will I get to do what I love every day, and be content?

Will I find the person I want to spend the rest of my life with? Will I fit into his family? Marriage is such a terrifying concept; leaving your childhood behind to start afresh with someone new. Will I be ready? When are you supposed to be ready?

5 years isn't so long away, but there's so much to do in such little time. There's so much to achieve. I can't wait to look back and be proud of myself. Will I even have the opportunity to look back and see how far I've come?

We'll have to wait and see.

Dear Future,
Here I am wondering about what'll happen in 5 years' time, but what will happen in 10 years' time? Let's fast forward time...

I imagine I'll be surrounded by miniature versions of myself running around and me struggling to deal with their naughtiness while I try to manage the house. Yeah, you got it right. I imagine I'll probably be a housewife. No, wait. The correct term is homemaker. Because I'll be creating a home for my husband and children to nourish and excel in. I'll be there motivating and encouraging the kids to become the best version of themselves.

And as much as I can picture that cute environment I'll be living in, I know there'll be total chaos at times. There'll be a lot of ups and downs.

In 10 years I will have grown a lot, I will have expanded my knowledge on things. I hope to become a stronger person than I am now. I am hoping the future holds good things for me.

I hope I am destined for great things.

I was once asked where I saw myself in 5 years' time. To be honest, at that time, I thought I'd have it all figured out. I thought I'd be studying the course I wanted in my preferred university. I thought I'd fall in love with my best friend and at the age of 21/22 I'd get married to him. I thought I'd have the career I'd always dreamed of. I thought I'd have it all. I thought I'd get it so easily. But everything is not what it seems. Life throws so many obstacles without you realizing. Nothing goes as planned. My goals for five years never came true. Not one. Most of my dreams didn't come true and I'm still working on the few I have left. I'm still working hard to have that dream ending because no matter what, I believe the ending will be a happy one. I may not know where I see myself in 5 years from now, but I know I'm working on my end goal. I'm ready for whatever life throws at me, regardless if its good or bad. I'm ready.

"If you had the chance, would you go back and change things. Or leave it as you are now?"

This question has been bugging me, pestering me at every corner of my brain. It's driving me insane. What would I do? Would I be asking myself this question if I knew? There's people I regret hurting, people I regret letting in. I've made mistakes, I'll admit it. There's nothing I want more in the world than to make peace with my past. To forget about things that didn't last. To stop looking over my shoulder, and move away from it all. But how can I when it haunts me in the dark of the night? I sit there wondering if I ever did anything right. I want to right all the wrongs, and go back to all that I've run from. I want to face it all head on. I want to forgive and be forgiven for all that I've done. But at that moment, I look back at how far I've come.

I've grown with each experience. I've strengthened as a person. Each person was a lesson, and I was just being tested. I try to look at the positives, as I have tried to all my life. I try to bring back that light that shined so brightly in my eyes. The same light that has been through all with me, that helped me see that some things are just not meant to be. every person I've lost or left behind, every chance I've missed or dismissed, every wish left unfulfilled. It was written in the stars, without a doubt. This is the way my life was meant to turn out. There's not much more I can do; I can't change what once was, but I can change what will be.

Life works in mysterious ways. And intentions are everything. Believe it or not, it determines the outcomes of your actions. Have good intentions, live a life you'll never regret. Hope for the best and never stray from your path.

I'm patiently waiting, waiting for the day, that things will eventually go my way. But it's easy to forget it all. it's easy to forget the reason behind the hardships, when life is treating you with such harshness. 'What have I done to deserve this?' I tell myself on a daily. But I see the small blessings that I've been receiving lately. It's the only reason why I haven't gone crazy. It's easy to tell someone to have hope, to have patience. It's also easy to fall into temptation. To forget the end goal for just a second. But sometimes it's what we need; it's a lesson. To help us go back on our paths stronger, with hope that we don't have to wait much longer. I'm waiting for you, and you're waiting for me. She's waiting in order to be the best she can be. They're waiting for the success and all they want is happiness. Maybe one comes without the other, or if you're lucky you'll get them together. Who's to say you can't have both? Just keep your head held high and let your tears dry. There's just a while to go, so don't be feeling so low. There are beautiful things that await you. No matter how hard things may seem at the moment, all I can say is never stop hoping.

I'm not saying I am perfect, for I am a book full of flaws. In every chapter, there's a part missing or untold. Secrets lie within each page, and the tears around the edges are visible. A book that has been torn in places you wouldn't believe, way before its years. A once smooth and presentable cover, now raggedy and rough. The writing is smudged from the tears and spills, where darkness took over for a while. The darkness never stops, but it never stops me from bringing in the light, shining it ever so bright. A candle of hope, a fragile and delicate substance guiding the way in times of need. No, I am not perfect nor do I strive to be. I just strive to be the best me I can be, and let those unwritten pages be filled with timeless happy memories; ones I can look back to and be proud of each and every single achievement. A book that's torn, battered and bent is a book with adventures, lessons and full of memories.

Dear future;
Yes, the future is scary.
Yes, the future is uncertain.
I don't know where it is I'm headed, what I'll do, who I'll be. It terrifies me that nothing is concrete, nothing is set in stone. Because anything can happen.
But that's the thing...
Anything can happen.
Anything can happen so make it the best experience you've ever had. Make it worthwhile.

Write a letter to your future self. Fill it with hopes and dreams you wish to fulfill. Fill it with happiness. Give yourself something to look forward to. And every now and then, look back and remind yourself of your goals. Remind yourself of the person you want to become.

- CHAPTER SEVEN –
DEAR YOU

DEAR YOU;

This is dedicated to you all; those that have supported me throughout my journey and have had a positive impact in my life. This gives me an opportunity to thank you for all that you have done, knowingly and unknowingly. This chapter is filled with incredible people with incredible hearts. You guys have been there for me in my good times and my bad, and I honestly can say I wouldn't want anyone else by my side throughout this journey.

There's too many people to thank, too many people who have stuck by me no matter what. Who have supported me. Too many to name. But just know that I am grateful for having people such amazing people in my life. Thank you all so much. I love each and every one of you.

Every time I thought I was at breaking point, and I couldn't go on; every time I thought I was at a loss, I was only gaining time and time again. I was gaining strength and love from those who are always there for me. I was gaining comfort from those who endlessly give me motivation to better myself. I was looking at the power of true friendship and the strength of true loved ones. Even when I thought my love for others were taken for granted, my angels showed me that they weren't worthy of my love. They didn't deserve the love I poured out unconditionally. I call them my angels because throughout my life, if and whenever I'm need of them, they are always there. True friends, real friends are like angels; the pure hearted, the strong, the honest. I am forever grateful for the support system I've gained by meeting these super amazing souls and all I ask is for Allah to reward them for their deeds, In Shaa Allah.

Darkness will leave my life, as long as I have you all by my side.

The hope and the love that has strengthened me, has only been from you. I have only managed to stay strong because of you. I am who I am today because of you.

Dear you.
All you wonderful people in my life.
There were so many times when I decided against this chapter simply because there were so many of you to thank.
But here it goes; a chapter dedicated to you.

First and foremost, thank you so much to every member of my family who have supported me through this journey of writing, for supporting my dreams and telling me to never give up on them. Thank you for giving me the motivation and inspiration I needed to finish this book. Thank you for bringing happiness and laughter in my life; a constant reminder that love is unconditional. I am so grateful to have such unique souls to call my siblings as each and every one of you are special to me. And I am grateful to have such caring and loving elder members in my family, always helping us grow into the people we are to become,

I love you all.

Dear all the elders in my family,
It wouldn't be right without thanking you all for bringing us up to become the people we are now. Each and every one of you had a part to play in bringing us all up. We all knew we had uncles and aunts and a grandmother to go to, as well as our parents.

My childhood consisted of being the centre of attention, because I was always able to get that attention. I had aunts and uncles and siblings and a grandmother all of whom adored me. I had parents giving me whatever I wanted. Even now, I see the love you all give us, and the life lessons we all get.

I am so grateful to have a family like ours; a support system that only grows with love. This will never be enough to show the gratitude I have for you all.

I hope I do you all proud one day, In Shaa Allah.

Dear my little babies;
My little siblings.
This is for each and every sibling in my family.
We have all grown up together, watching all of us grow
into smart, mature children. No matter what, we'll still
be the babies of the family. The elders will never let us
hear the end of our embarrassing stories and we all
know I have too many to count.

To this day, I don't know why but you all seem to look
up to me. You all admire me and it makes me so happy
that you do. I remember as little kids, I used to make
you all play my make-believe games and you would
somehow go along with it. We're still so close, even
though we're all years apart. And you guys are so
supportive of me regardless of what it is. And I guess
that's what family is; being supportive of one another
no matter what.

Dear Taj,

Bet you never saw this coming... you didn't, did you?
Well, I'm hoping you end up reading this, because this is
about how much you mean to me.

Well... where to start? We've known each other since I
was little; first as neighbours and then as something
more as the years went by. We used to always have
sleepovers, and play games with each other as we grew
up. You were this older, cooler cousin I always had and I
always looked up to you.

As we grew up, I could see the strong, independent
person you were turning out to be. And I admired that.
You had confidence, intelligence, and I strived to be like
you for so long. And in some ways, I still do. You've
achieved so much already and I am so proud of you. I
am so proud of who you've become. And I am so
grateful for having you in my life for so long.

I remember that evening where me, you and Afsana sat
in your house ranting about life and everything; where
you gave me the confidence to take control of my life
and do what I was scared to do for so long. You've
always advised me, scolded me and comforted me at
the right times. You've never made me feel like I was
alone; you've supported me with so much. I just wish I
do the same for you, in the ways you do for me.

I love our chats together, and outings and our gossip

sessions. I remember the day you came up with the word 'PAT' and since then you've always called me that. But I hope after reading this you realise why I am your 'PAT'. Because I want to be as strong and as confident as you. I admire all that you are and all that you do and I wish you get everything you deserve from now on. I hope you get all the happiness you want in life. And know, I am always here for you.

Dear Rabiah,
If someone told me that the little girl in my
Nursery/Reception class would become one of my
closest friends when I grow up, I'd look at them with
amazement only because I wouldn't really understand
what they're saying (I was 3/4 you know!). But honestly,
I don't think either of us saw this coming.

We have such an unusual relationship it sometimes
baffles me; we're so comfortable with each other,
nothing seems weird. We talk about the most random
things that we don't even get.

I am so grateful that I got to meet you again in college,
years after primary school; I am so grateful fate led me
back to you. You've taught me so much. We've both
seen the transformation in myself in the last couple of
years and it's mainly because of you. You helped me
grow stronger, and not let things get to me. You
strengthened me. Thank you so so so much.

You always tell me you're the harsh one, but I've need
that harsh figure in my life; you became a mum figure
and looked after me like I was your child (which is odd
because I'm the older one).

Continue to be the strong minded person I know that
you are. I know you can achieve your dreams, you're
determined enough to do it. Just don't ever give up on
them.

Dear Sadia,
Oh wow, I can already feel the emotions flooding in and
I haven't even started...
Let's start with the story we always seem to retell when
we reminisce about our time together, especially on
birthdays.

It was a bright, sunny morning the day we met; (I can't
remember if it was bright that day... or sunny.. or in fact
the morning...) I walked into the Law class and I see you
sitting all alone and so I walked over to you with the
biggest smile, and start talking to you as if I knew you
already. I know we always joke about how bubbly I was
that day, but I'm glad I was. Because it was the start of
the most beautiful friendship. AS Law was the reason
for our friendship and the love I had for you just grew
over the years.

It's been nearly four years since we first met, and we've
been through so much together. We really have. It's
actually funny because I was only with you at college for
a year and the rest of the three years we barely saw
each other, yet our bond has stayed so strong. We
compromised, and sacrificed, and we got here. We did
it.

It's hard to say that about a lot of friendships; that the
bond has still stayed strong after being apart for a
while, but every time we meet it's like nothing's
changed.

You've been there through all the tears and all the
happiness in my life. And you've been giving me endless
advice on life, and how to become the independent

woman I need to be. You've given me the strength to believe that I can be that woman. I can get through things and move on. I can be strong.

I hope this friendship of ours remains even when were married and have kids, like we always joke about. Because I can see us now, talking on the phone, complaining about the same old things and meeting up for catch-up sessions.

Life wouldn't be the same without your obsession with Justin Bieber and your singing that never seems to stop when we see each other. Or our Facetime calls and random chats in the night. The memories I've made with you are ones that I'll treasure for years to come.

Thank you so much for everything, for your support and motivation, for being you.

Dear Jubran (@akhthatwritess),
I haven't known you long, but I guess time doesn't measure a bond like ours. This is for you, because you've been there for me, helping me with endless advice and endless support. You're more like an older sibling, with your protectiveness, even though you're younger than me, but I guess we both have that protectiveness for each other, like real siblings.

Things may seem dark at times and I know it gets you down, but I know you have a bright future ahead of you. I know you have the potential to do so much more. You just have to believe in yourself and believe that you can do it. From what I know, life hasn't been too great, but you can turn it around. There's still time. And I know that you can do it.

We don't talk as much these days, but it doesn't change how we are with each other. We'll always ask after each other, checking up to see if the other is okay. I don't know how we came to have such a strong sibling bond but I'm glad I have you in my life.

Thank you so much Jubs, you've been there for me and helped me so much. I cannot put into words how grateful I am to have someone like you, always looking out for me. You've proved time and time again that you've always got my back. Like I said, you're like my older brother, not my younger brother. I have so much love for you honestly.

I wish nothing but the best for you and your future.

Dear Ra'naa (@innerrambling),

I'm hoping you didn't see this coming, so it comes as a surprise to you and I get to make you cry (happy tears of course).

So, before I became your friend, I was simply one of your followers on Instagram. And you were this big writer who was obsessed with pineapples. Even before I created my account, I used to follow you from my personal. You're one of my favourite writers; you inspire people to believe in themselves and love themselves. It's one of the things I admire about you.

We never used to talk as much before, we never took time to get to know each other. But you came back after a long break from Instagram and that was the start of our beautiful friendship. I remember when we wrote our first collab together and to this day, it's one of my favourite collabs.

We've gotten so close over the past year and I can honestly say that you have been so supportive of me and have helped me through so much. I know if there is anything troubling me, you'd know exactly what to do and what to say. And like you always say, you're more than a friend. You're a sister to me. You've helped me through so many problems, supported me in times where I felt I was alone and you never let me feel like that for long. Over the past few months, you've also been like a mother to me. You took care of me; checking up on me when you felt something was wrong.

And I am ever so grateful to have someone like you in my life.

I wish you nothing but happiness, Ra'naa. You deserve it. You've helped so many people get back up from dark places, and I don't ever want you to go through any more than you already have. You've shown us all your strength, and your ability to move forward with life. I hope you're always smiling and spreading laughter with your jokes.

Lastly, thank you to everyone that's been so supportive of me and the writing process of this book; it hasn't been easy, there's honestly so many of you to name but I have so much love for the Instagram family, all my friends from secondary, college and university. I know there's a lot of people I am not close to but they have also been so supportive, so thank you so much. Without all this support from everyone, *Dear You* wouldn't have been possible.

Dear you,
We all need support and motivation from our loved
ones. It gives us the strength to go on. We all need
people fighting in our corner, helping us through the
struggles of life. We all need that person, and we need
to become that person for someone.

Don't take them for granted because one day you'll lose
them because of your half'-heartedness or
stubbornness, and you'll realise that you've lost a good
person. No one wants that.

Hold on tight, and never give them a reason to let go.

Thank you, dear reader, for following me through this journey; for opening the memoirs of a lost penguin.
I hope reading this has benefitted you in one way or another.

Nishat B. Ahmed
(@n.a.writes)

Made in the USA
Lexington, KY
16 May 2018